REDUCE, REUSE AND RECYCLE

THE SECRET TO ENVIRONMENTAL SUSTAINABILITY

ENVIRONMENT TEXTBOOKS
Children's Environment Books

BABY PROFESSOR
EDUCATION KIDS

Speedy Publishing LLC
40 E. Main St. #1156
Newark, DE 19711
www.speedypublishing.com

In this book, we're going to talk about doing your part to help the environment by reducing, reusing, and recycling. So, let's get right to it!

Fifty billion cans are thrown out every year in the United States. Over 25 billion glass containers are thrown out too. About 1/3 of the garbage we throw out in the trash every week is materials that are used to package things we buy. Where does all this garbage end up? Most of it will end up in a landfill.

After it's buried, it will take hundreds of years for it to decompose. In fact, some types of materials, such as glass, will take thousands of years to break down.

As the population grows and our stacks of garbage grow, we need more and more landfill space. By following a practice of reducing what you use, reusing things where you can, and recycling as much as possible, you can decrease the amount of your garbage that goes to landfills.

Garbage waste dumped in landfill site.

Convenient but unhealthy polystyrene lunch boxes with take away.

REDUCE

One of the ways you can help save the environment is by reducing the amount of things that you buy as well as the waste that you throw out.

WATCH THE AMOUNT OF PACKAGING YOU BUY

Look carefully at the things you buy and try not to buy things that have packaging that can't be recycled. There are so many grocery and other consumer products that use an excess amount of packaging. Fast food restaurants are big offenders here. They frequently package their foods in foam containers, made of a substance called polystyrene, and plastics. It's healthier to eat at home, but when you do eat out, try to pick places that use ecofriendly packaging and make an effort to use materials that can be recycled.

Styrofoam Boxes.

BORROW INSTEAD OF BUY, ESPECIALLY FOR BIG-TICKET ITEMS

If you're not going to use something very much, see if you can find a way to borrow it or rent it instead of buying it. For example, power tools or regular household tools you need might be a good case of something you could borrow instead of buy.

If you need suitcases for an upcoming trip, but you don't travel that often, borrowing them might be a good idea. Camping equipment and sports equipment is expensive and takes up a lot of space, so it might be best to borrow it instead of purchasing it.

GET RID OF YOUR GAS-POWERED CAR OR DRIVE IT LESS

Cars that use gasoline cause a lot of pollution. If you live someplace where you can walk to places, your family might not need a car at all. If it's not possible for your family to be without a car, you may want to talk to your parents about buying an electric car the next time they purchase a car.

Electric Car in Charging Station.

Electric cars are a lot less polluting than cars powered by gasoline. There may be times when you can walk or take the bus. Riding a bike is good exercise and doesn't produce any pollution like a car does.

Electric car at charging station.

THINK ABOUT BUYING AND USING A COMPOST BIN

You can begin using a compost bin. If you have a large enough yard, you can buy a plastic bin that is especially designed for composting. There's a science to the proper composting. You can throw away certain types of materials and if you mix them properly you can use them as a fertilizer later for your lawn and plants. If you do it the right way, you'll have a lot less to throw out weekly meaning that you won't be filling up a landfill.

Compost in wooden box.

You can throw leaves and any type of grass clippings in. You can also throw in all non-animal types of food scraps, such as banana peels, leftover bread or cereal, and grounds from coffee and tea. Bedding from animals that are herbivores and organic manure are okay too. Dry cat or dog food and dust from cleaning up can be added in as well.

Garden Compost Bin.

There are other types of items you can add in, such as shredded newspaper or wood chips, but they may not decompose for quite some time. The types of items you really shouldn't put in are pet droppings or animal products like meat, bones, or fish skins.

Compost in the garden.

USE A COMPUTER TO READ MAGAZINES AND NEWSPAPERS

Most magazines as well as newspapers have online versions now so you don't need to get print versions. You can read books on your computer and other handheld devices too. Be careful how much paper you use at home. Paper that you use in your home printer and paper towels in the kitchen can become extra waste.

News on digital tablet.

SAVE ENERGY BY TURNING OFF LIGHTS

When you're going out of a room or rooms for a while, turn off the lights to reduce energy consumption.

AVOID OVEREATING AND WASTING FOOD

Over 35% of the food we buy in the United States, gets thrown out and then goes into a landfill. Try to buy just what you need and eat what you buy.

Turn off the light.

REDUCE THE WATER YOU USE EVERY DAY

In areas where there are droughts, the people who live there have learned how to save water. If you think about the water you use every day, there are lots of ways to use less. Some of the ways to save water are very simple. Keep showers short and don't stay under the water for more than 5 minutes.

Limited resource of water.

Most people stay in the shower for 10-15 minutes and use a lot more water than they need to. Don't leave the water running while you brush your teeth. Watch your water consumption for a month or more and then look at your water bill to see if you're using less water.

GET OFF THE JUNK MAIL LISTS

More than 100,000,000,000 junk mail pieces are placed in mailboxes in the United States every year. You can stop receiving these mailings and get off the lists. Do some research online to find out who to contact to get off these lists for a five year period of time or permanently.

Junk Mail Leaflets.

Group of recycled cans.

REUSE

Another way you can help the environment is by reusing things instead of throwing them out. You'd be surprised what you can reuse if you get creative.

USE CLOTH BAGS INSTEAD OF PAPER OR PLASTIC

Instead of using paper bags or plastic bags at the grocery store when you shop try using cloth bags that you can store and use over and over again. They work better than paper or plastic for carrying groceries, which is an added benefit.

USE REUSABLE LUNCH BOXES OR PLASTIC CONTAINERS

Instead of using paper that you'll need to throw out, use a reusable lunch box with plastic containers that you can wash out to bring your lunch to school.

REUSE CONTAINERS INSTEAD OF THROWING THEM OUT

Coffee cans, plastic tubs, shoeboxes, and egg cartons can be cleaned out and used for storage or fun crafts. Coffee cans are great for storing nails, screws, or buttons and egg cartons are perfect for collections of small shells or rocks.

Cotton shopping bag overflowing with vegetables.

DONATE USABLE ITEMS THAT YOU DON'T WANT ANYMORE

Instead of throwing out old clothes or old toys, donate them. Old furniture and other household items can be donated too. You'll get a tax deduction if you get a receipt for the items you donated. You can have a yard sale too if you need some cash

Clothing donation box.

USE WASHABLE DISHES AND SILVERWARE

Instead of using paper plates and plastic forks or spoons that will have to be thrown away once they're used, use regular dishes and silverware for your meals.

USE PAPER MORE THAN ONCE

If you use writing paper, put it into a bin when one side is used, so that someone can take it and use it on the other side.

Green maple leaf with recycle symbol.

RECYCLE

When you recycle materials, it means that less material is going into landfills and instead is being reused again to create new products. Since these materials are going to be used again, it means that we don't need to take more of Earth's resources to make them. Recycling cuts down on pollution in the environment as well.

WHAT DOES THE RECYCLING SYMBOL MEAN?

The recycling symbol contains three arrows arranged in a loop. Each arrow represents a different step in the recycling process. In the first step, we collect the materials to be recycled. Lots of different types of products can be recycled now. Here's a partial list:

- Plastics of all types

- Glass containers of all sizes

Father and child taking out recycle trash.

- Paper, most types can be recycled

- Cloth

- Metals of all types

- Computers

- Batteries

Cardboard bundles for recycling.

The next step is the old recycled materials are processed to make new products. The last step is to watch for items that are made of recycled materials when you buy again.

Battery recycling concept.

Family cleans up their community park.

Instead of throwing things into the trash, try to recycle as much as possible. If you have a recycling can that's picked up every week or two at your house, read your city's recycling guidelines and recycle as much as you can.

Awesome! Now you know more about the different things you can do to help save the environment by reducing, reusing, and recycling. You can find more Environment books from Baby Professor by searching the website of your favorite book retailer.

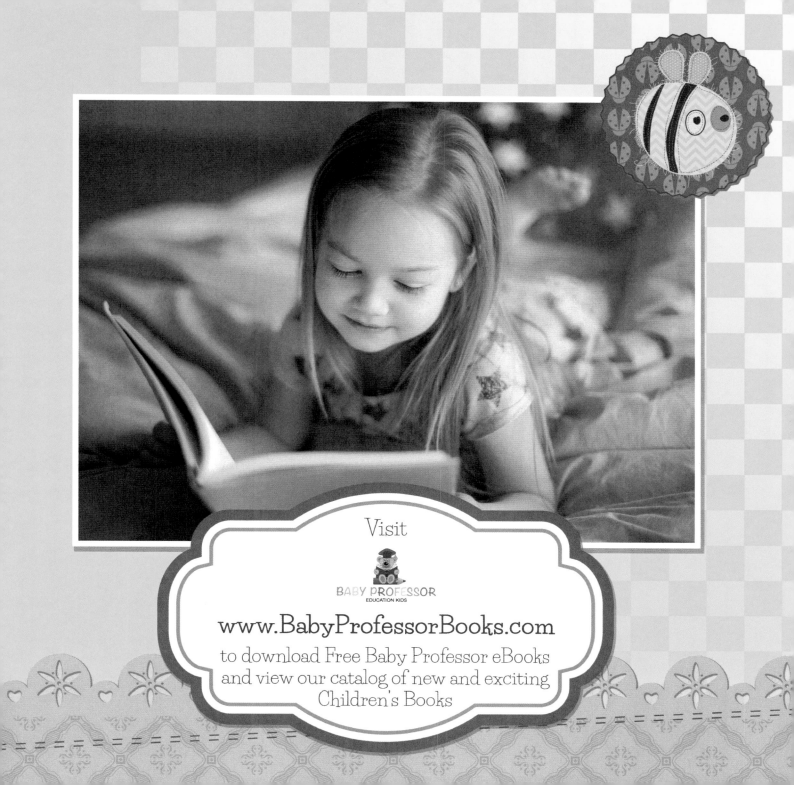

Visit

BABY PROFESSOR
EDUCATION KIDS

www.BabyProfessorBooks.com

to download Free Baby Professor eBooks
and view our catalog of new and exciting
Children's Books